Life As Taught Me By My Professors & My Jewish Mother

By Paul B. Lowney

Informative, philosophic and humorous commentaries on the human experience and the universe we live in.

Design & typography by Spencer Rossman

LITTLE LESSONS FROM LIFE

CROWNE AND LURIE PUBLISHERS

Copyright 1999
Paul B. Lowney, Seattle, Washington
All rights reserved
ISBN 0-9609946-5-3
Library of Congress Catalog Card Number: 96-094898
Printed in the United States of America

Other books by Paul Lowney: (hardbacks) *Offbeat Humor, The Best in Offbeat Humor, The Best in Offbeat Humor II, The Love Game, Gleeb, The Big Book of Gleeb, Toads, No Charge for Dreaming*; (paperbacks) *This is Hydroplaning, Seattle – the Nation's Most Beautiful City, The Best of Gleeb, The Pocket Gleeb, Toads – Expanded Edition*.

LITTLE LESSONS FROM LIFE

Laughter
has no foreign accent.

LITTLE LESSONS FROM LIFE

The deepest cut of all is to be rejected by someone you don't want.

LITTLE LESSONS FROM LIFE

People tell you to have a nice day, but they never explain how to do it.

LITTLE LESSONS FROM LIFE

*O*ur attitude toward life attracts the realities of life to match that attitude.

LITTLE LESSONS FROM LIFE

Should marriage licenses expire if they are not renewed every two years?

Some marriages don't work out, but on the other hand, some divorces don't work out, either.

For those of you who keep saying, "I'm trying to find myself," here's some advice: Mail a letter to yourself and then follow the postman.

Nutritionists claim that if you include whole grains in your daily diet, you'll live longer – that is, if you don't get murdered.

Many of the same foods are both good and bad for you, so be warned: Eating can be dangerous to your health. (Not eating can also be dangerous to your health.)

When we're in love, we see good in the person; when love ends, we see faults.

According to theory, plants thrive better if you talk to them in soft, loving tones. Does this mean that you can kill weeds by screaming obscenities at them?

If someone starts looking more attractive to you, it may not be a change in that person. It could be that as you move along in life, you're lowering your standards.

To form a good habit, don't make exceptions. To break a bad habit, make exceptions.

Older people who dress and groom like the young, generally end up looking like older people trying to look young.

If the doctor gives you a placebo pill and you forget to take it, but you think you did, you'll get the same effect.

He said that the new battery for his quartz watch would last a long, long time because he seldom looks at his watch.

There must be more to life than recorded messages.

LITTLE LESSONS FROM LIFE

Meditation will help you relieve stress. It works best if you're not stressed.

In five billion years the sun will begin running out of fuel. This thermonuclear burnout will expand the sun 100 times its original size and will turn Earth into a scorched planetary corpse. You can make plans for this disaster right now, or you can be the type of person who waits until the last minute.

The remotest object detected in the universe is a galaxy more than 12.2 billion light years from Earth. *Far out!* The densest object is a collapsed giant star in a black hole state which weighs trillions of tons per cubic inch. *Heavy!* This density causes a gravitational force so powerful that it holds back light, thus making a black hole invisible. *Out of sight!*

People have a right to their own opinion, but the right to an opinion doesn't ensure merit for an opinion. That's because some opinions just aren't worth a damn.

LITTLE LESSONS FROM LIFE

A house is not a home if there's no peanut butter.

There are times when you may want to say to a person, "Is this the real you or is it Prozac, Paxil, or Zoloft?"

Honesty with those you care about should not be used as a dagger to draw blood, but as a lantern to give light when darkness serves no purpose.

Like my mother always said, "If you promise to do something, do it – don't think that if you can find an excuse good enough, it's all right not to do it."

If you try and try and try and the relationship doesn't work out, solve the problem with your coat – put it on and clear out.

Friendship growing into love can make you happy, but love growing into friendship can make you sad.

If a man and woman start out as lovers and then end up as friends, what does it mean? It means that one of them was dumped.

Our mental and physical states are constantly shifting and changing, and the world "out there" that we react to is constantly shifting and changing, so how do we know for certain that at any given moment our judgments of our life situations are reliable?

Knowing how to receive graciously is a form of giving.

A person who keeps his word is like a rock; a person who doesn't keep his word is like a shadow.

The more secure you feel, the easier it is to admit when you're wrong – and vice versa.

There is no difference between being in love and thinking you're in love – the joy and the pain are the same.

Pursuing a losing love affair is like tightening your hand into a fist until your knuckles turn white. Letting go is like opening your hand. It feels better, but it's empty.

There's another side to the expression: "Go ahead and do it – you only live once." It's this: If you want to get the most out of the life which you "only live once," there are some things you must decide against.

She said to him: "You certainly don't look, act, and sound like you're 67," and he said: "I, myself, am not, but parts of me are."

One problem with life is that the mind is not the same as the body. The mind can wish for our being to be fulfilled, and to be well and strong, and free of pain, and to gratify desire, and to be loved, and to do wonderful things; but the body may not support these wishes. The mind has freedom, but does not exist freely. You might say that the mind is a prisoner of the body. And conversely, the body is a prisoner of the mind. The mind – if it is well and happy – can help the body, but if it is sick or despaired, it can harm the body.

Ergo: A psychosomatic approach to life is desirable.

LITTLE LESSONS FROM LIFE

If you do not accept the imperfections of your loved one, you do not love at all.

LITTLE LESSONS FROM LIFE

If you don't feel like yourself, is it possible you're somebody else?

Most people believe that life is not a waste of time.

Some people talk a lot to cover up their reticence, and some people act bold to conceal their shyness, and some people act conceited to hide their inferiority complex, and some people act friendly to mask their hostility, and some people act intellectual to cover up their ignorance.

Ergo: Does this mean that anything you can act, you can be?

To prove your view of life is merely a matter of perspective, consider bicycling. When you're riding a bicycle, you say to yourself, "Move your stupid cars out of my way," and when you're driving a car, you say to yourself, "Can't you find some other place to ride your dumb bicycle?"

She lies only if the truth is too painful to someone or to herself. All things considered, you can make a good case for this type of lying.

We are breathing-in millions of electromagnetic waves that are flying through the air from wireless phones, beepers, radio and television stations, and man-made satellites. It is quite possible that we could breathe-in a football game or even an obscene phone call.

ANCIENT BACTERIA, 250 MILLION years old, were found in ice crystals and were revived, claim microbiologists. They don't explain how it is possible for life to exist this long, so the question is: What is the composition of the divine spark we call life – a spark that humans, with all their knowledge and genius, cannot create one cell of it in the laboratory? And if a bit of life is 250 million years old, what has it been doing all this time? Also, what is it that's in a simple bacterium that makes it alive as opposed to what's missing in a bacterium that makes it dead? Answers, please. Anyone?

If a psychiatrist prescribes tranquilizers for your depression, you'll probably end up a relaxed, depressed person.

Generally speaking, a misanthrope is more socially acceptable than a bigot.

An act of generosity toward a person may contain a certain amount of selfishness. Reason? There could be an advantage in having that person feel obligated.

If rabbit tastes like chicken, and if pheasant tastes like chicken, and if frog legs taste like chicken, and if turtle tastes like chicken, then why do we keep picking on the chickens?

In life, you're more likely to get what you expect rather than what you want.

If you can't make good, make good excuses works the least when used the most.

HERE'S A BIT OF INFORMATION you'll probably never use unless you're talking about fish: Marvel at the fecundity of the Atlantic cod and at Nature's balancing act. A large cod can lay 5 million eggs, 99 percent of which are eaten by predators, and out of the 1 percent remaining, 90 percent never reach maturity. If the survival rate were much higher, the cod population would move toward unsustainable infinity. If the survival rate were much less, the cod would vanish.

The leading cause of unhappiness is loneliness, and this results mainly from social isolation. Everyone, at some time or other, experiences this condition.

There is a difference between attitude and prejudice. Attitude is based on what a person does; prejudice is based on what a person is.

LITTLE LESSONS FROM LIFE

The antonym of synonym is antonym.

LITTLE LESSONS FROM LIFE

If you don't like life, is there a reasonable alternative?

A bored person is one who says, "I wish I were hungry so I could eat."

At dinner, my mother said to us children: "When there's food on the table, eat, don't talk, and if you must talk, then talk friendly, but don't argue; and if you must argue, do it while you're washing dishes."

To make your life seem longer, travel a lot. New things in new places give you a kaleidoscopic effect and stretch life, but the same things in the same places give you a snapshot effect and compress life.

He said he didn't particularly like traveling, but he traveled quite often, because he claimed it was the only way he could enjoy coming back home.

If God were to send a message in three words to all peoples on Earth, what would those three words be? Most likely, *Love one another* or *Live in peace* – probably *Love one another.*

A sentence written by author/philosopher Ashleigh Brilliant is worth repeating: "Surely I deserve some kind of recognition for all the bad things I haven't done."

Astronaut Edgar Mitchell made this perceptive observation: "There are no supernatural phenomena, only very large gaps in our knowledge of what is natural."

LITTLE LESSONS FROM LIFE

What's the meaning of life? To find out, go into the wilderness for three days – take nothing with you – and you will learn the meaning. Survival.

What does the brain think about to get itself to think of something?

When love works out, it brings joy. When love doesn't work out, it brings pain, so be warned: *Loving someone could prove hazardous to your health.*

LITTLE LESSONS FROM LIFE

*L*ook for a good love, and if you can't find one, look for a good substitute.

Some people won't give up coffee because they don't want to face life all by themselves.

IF YOU'RE DEPRESSED, THERE'S little point in people telling you things like: *Every cloud has a silver lining... It's always darkest before the dawn... You'll feel better in the morning... Count your blessings... Think positive ... Chin up...* These are nice-sounding stereotypes, but probably have no bearing on your problems.

Don't confuse truth with honesty. Truth is the purest form of reality. Honesty strives for truth, but too often it is crippled by bias.

A famous holistic doctor said: "If you don't hurt, you don't change. Pain is God's reset button."

There's a common impulse that embraces all life forms: If it feels good, do more of it; if it feels bad, don't do it.

The reason older people are wiser – not necessarily smarter – than younger people is that they've already experienced a series of life situations, and like seeing reruns of old movies, they know the outcome. To put it into philosophical terms, you might say that the older have the advantage of a priori (based on reason) and empirical (based on experience) versus only a priori for the younger. Think of it this way: If you were to be led through the hazardous swamps of the Everglades, whom would you rather have as a guide – an old timer who spent a lifetime traveling through the swamps or a student just out of college with a degree in swampology?

Before you show up at an important social event, check the mirror first so you'll know how much confidence to have.

No one completely owns his own life. Everyone – no matter how insignificant – has an effect on someone else, just as a stone sends out ripples when thrown into still water. A person whose life doesn't touch another's is a person without a shadow.

LITTLE LESSONS FROM LIFE

A harmless lie is harmful when you're caught at it.

LITTLE LESSONS FROM LIFE

It isn't boasting when you refuse to let modesty stand in the way of the facts.

When they broke up, he said, "You'll find someone else, and we can still be friends… and you've taught me a lot: kindness, compassion, understanding, caring," and she said, "Thanks, and you've taught me a lot, too: lying, cheating, arrogance, insensitivity, and selfishness."

Why is it that love between man and woman can be so rewarding and all-consuming, and yet can be so destructive and painful? For an answer, consider these words from actor George Burns, playing the role of God: *I could never figure out how to make anything with just one side to it. You ever see a front without a back? A top without a bottom? An up without a down?* To his words, add this: For the happiness of mutual love – if lost – there is pain.

Allow yourself extra time for any unexpected contingency, and you'll be on time consistently, but you'll risk being early.

When a person continually says, "I'm busy," does "busy" mean a fixed, objective condition or is it rather a subjective prioritization of time?

You hate the mountain because it blocks the sun, and then you awake one morning and find the mountain is gone; and then you realize you loved the mountain. You didn't know it because it was always there.

THREE YOUNG MEN WENT TO a house party. Two of them said they didn't have a good time because they said the women were older and unattractive. The third one said he had a good time. His expectations were lower.

Chasing after fun and good times as a main goal in life is self-defeating. A more realistic goal is to make something of yourself and do good things for others and yourself, and then fun and good times will come to you as a by-product... Somewhat in the same vein is this: A young singer asked a famous operatic baritone how he could become a successful singer, and the opera star answered: "Be less concerned about being a successful singer; be more concerned about being a good singer."

Regardless of how trivial the achievement, a person is not a failure if he fulfills the highest measure of his potential, but a person with a high potential and trivial fulfillment is.

LITTLE LESSONS FROM LIFE

We generally approve of those people who have the courage of our convictions.

If you are the host for an evening out, and you have a miserable time, pay your bill with cash instead of using your credit card. That way, you won't relive the whole thing in 30 days.

ISN'T NATURE WONDERFUL? But we can't always let Nature have her way. Nature gave us a brain that we can use to outwit and tame Nature. If Nature had her own way, she'd do-us-in at an early age.

If you are sick of all the suffering and pain on this planet, you can always move to another planet, unless, of course, you can't get the time off from work.

The familiar saying, "You're only as old as you feel," is only half true. The other half is, "You're only as old as people around you make you feel."

Regardless of what we are supposed to do or what's expected of us, we generally end up doing what we really want to do, and then we offer reasons to justify what we did.

In any mortal conflict, don't we generally believe that God is on the side we sympathize with?

IF YOU DON'T WANT TO BE A conversational bore, don't go into lengthy detail on subjects that the listener has no share or interest in, and get to the point. There are exceptions, of course, such as verbalizing a lot of private feelings that need an outlet; and if this is the case, you can say: "I know this may be boring to you, but I just have to tell someone; and besides, I want to hear it myself."

Which is more important in life – the journey or the destination? When you are young, it is the destination; when you are older, the destination is the journey.

In a view of our distant future, we at present are ancients and all our works are antiquities – and in a view of the future, not so distant, what is *in* today is *out* tomorrow; and what is *hip* and *cool* today is *old fashioned* and *corny* tomorrow, so perhaps it is wiser not to embrace wholeheartedly the aberrations of the *now, pop* culture as lasting realities, for these aberrations are merely ephemeral bubbles on the endless river of life that could lead to discomfort and scorn.

LITTLE LESSONS FROM LIFE

ISN'T IT OBVIOUS
that the same people who can make us happy can make us unhappy?

Whenever his ego suffered, he went to socials where the people were dull and unattractive so he could stand around feeling superior.

Loyalty to a person shouldn't be so strong that it blinds you to the truth about that person. You can accept the truth and still be loyal, if you choose.

HOW DO WE KNOW THAT THE impressions our senses deliver to our brain are the same as the matter it senses? For instance, our senses tell us that the point of a pin is smooth and sharp, but a microscope would show the point to be jagged and dull. An electron microscope might show the pin teeming with bacteria, and a more powerful microscope could simply show molecules; and if it were possible to break down the molecules, we could end up with the elemental building blocks of matter – quarks. So what is the reality of the pin – what our ordinary senses convey to our brain or what the pin is in its ultimate reality? Our senses are fragile, inconsistent and unreliable, so, from the standpoint of ordinary human observation, the true nature of matter "out there" is incomplete and perhaps unknowable.

Ergo: Leave a measure of doubt in your certainty of the world around you.

If you are overly intent on wanting something to happen, there's a good chance it won't; and if you are overly fearful something will happen, there is a good chance it will.

People who take a short package tour of several neighboring countries may miss a few countries if they don't have a seat by the window.

LITTLE LESSONS FROM LIFE

There are many people whose outstanding characteristic is that they go unnoticed.

A dandelion farmer found tulips growing in his field. He ripped them out and said, "Weeds are such a nuisance."

The four forces of the universe are electromagnetism, gravity, the strong force, and the weak force; and the six quarks are top, bottom, up, down, charm, and strange. And also: A variety of plankton called dinoflagellate is both plant and animal. It's a plant because it manufactures its own food, and it's an animal because it has the power of self-locomotion. What good is this information? It could be useful to you if someone ever asks, "What do you know?"

If you are lost in the forest, it's possible to stay alive by eating earthworms, but then you run the risk of being attacked by robins.

A psychotherapist may not cure your neuroses, but at least you'll learn how to hide yours and to recognize them in others.

A person caught in a lie and then denies the lie, doubles the lie.

This is a most peculiar planet. Everyone is eating everyone. Creatures big and small eat one another. Animals eat animals; fish eat one another, and so do insects; and so do some birds; and humans eat most any creature that tastes good and is digestible. A man ate a mother sparrow, and the newborn baby sparrow said, "I'm hungry. Someone ate my mother." *Vegetarianism seems to be the kindest approach to life.*

The entire universe began in a vacuum with the explosion of a tiny speck of infinitely hot and dense matter, so the question is: Where did the speck come from? Since this knowledge is beyond human comprehension, the answer is: Who cares?

A neutron star is an extremely dense, collapsed star that has stopped short of becoming a black hole. A tablespoon of it weighs about 40 billion tons. If you ever happen to see a small piece of a neutron star that has accidentally fallen to Earth, you are to heed this warning: It could be exceedingly hot, so don't pick it up.

If you're ever sucked into a black hole, you'll travel through it at the speed of light and you won't age, but on the other hand, you won't have any fun.

In a conversation, you may forget what you were going to say next if you concentrate too much on what the other person is saying.

Her bonsai tree was terminally ill, and she wanted to give it a transfusion, but she couldn't find a donor with the right sap type.

Little Lessons From Life

An extensive study of current studies found that many studies are flawed because of errors in compiling statistical data and because of unscientific application of controls – but a later study claimed that this particular study drew false conclusions.

The most complex, ingenuous structure in the entire known universe is the human brain. It was built by cellular mutation in a trial-and-error process using an enormous expanse of time, probably 3½ billion years. If Nature – without a brain – built a brain with the tools of trial and error and enormous time, what does it tell us? It tells us that possibly there is some type of unknown, guiding intelligence locked into infinite time, and that given enough time, all things seem to be possible; and it tells us that eventually, a human brain can do what Nature did – build a brain. For those seeking an easy explanation for all this, there is always, "God did it."

In human relations, life is a continuum of quid pro quo. We are all engaged in giving and getting. Like an unseen adhesive, this process of mutual benefit binds us together; but if either the giving or the getting fails, then the binding comes apart and the quid pro quo dissolves, and then it's on to the next quid pro quo.

If you believe that inside beauty is more important than outside beauty, then don't judge people by their photographs. Judge them by their CAT scans.

LITTLE LESSONS FROM LIFE

A well-known U.S. senator remarked that this country is the best in technology and the worst in raising children. Think about this: Many of our famous leaders were reared in the old-fashioned philosophy of RR– Reasonable Repression. Children lack the experience and judgment to do everything they want to do, and everything they feel like doing, without causing harm to themselves or others.

LITTLE LESSONS FROM LIFE

In olden times, slaves made life easier for their masters. In modern times, slaves do the same, and they don't need housing or sleep, and all they eat is a little bit of electricity. They are called computers.

Of all the Earth's life-forms, modern humans are the only ones who retire. Considering the totality of all life, it's obvious that work is an essential meaning of existence.

A zoo is a penitentiary for animals. Their sentence: Life without parole. Their crime: Being weaker than their captors.

If, for humane reasons, you don't believe in eating the flesh of animals, there's a way to do it and not feel guilt. Apply *The Principle of Just Compensation.* Eat only the animals that are killers, such as lions, tigers, leopards, coyotes, weasels, eagles, owls, snakes, and alligators.

He lived alone in the wilderness and he ate plants and animals, but he didn't believe in killing the animals, so he taught them to commit suicide.

Science fiction: Contrary to the assertion that infinity cannot be measured, there is a way: Measure halfway from the beginning and then multiply by two.

With the intelligence to constantly improve – and given infinite time – humans will imperceptibly move toward perfection, until at some point they will become one and intuitive with the ultimate. This could be the final understanding and the Grand Design of Life.

LITTLE LESSONS FROM LIFE

After humans evolved an intelligent, questioning brain, they began searching for answers to the mysteries of life surrounding them, and because this searching needed satisfaction, they created God as a source of answers, so it didn't matter whether God did or did not exist. It mattered only that the inquiring human brain found resolution in the exercise of searching and finding. Will God ever reveal himself to humans to prove he exists? God only knows.